KINI SMOON

YOU ARE NOT ALONE

I0558988

published by IAmEncouragement, LLC
ISBN-13: 979-8-9891660-5-3

Contents

CHAPTER 1

NO WAY
BUT OUT

In the claustrophobic abyss of my mind, I found myself entombed. The towering walls of self-doubt, like jagged cliffs, loomed over me, casting long shadows of fear upon my soul. Every word, every glance, every flicker of an eyelid, echoed in the deafening silence of my prison. I longed to escape, to break free from the shackles that bound me, but the weight of my past held me captive. "Shine, you can't keep hiding from the world," my grandfather's voice whispered. "You are meant for more, my child." The words echoed in the desolate wasteland of my mind, but I turned away, seeking refuge in the familiar darkness that consumed me. In this desolate realm. Have you ever been in a desolate realm? A space where you thought you had to stay? Things aren't going the way that they should. Questions you can't get answered. Places you can't seem to go. People you can't see. Jobs you can't get. And you say there is no way on God's green earth this could be happening to me!! Well, guess what friend? We're in this together. Allow me to introduce myself, hey, my name is Shine. Let me tell you what's been going on.

Life was going well. I was working and making money. I was in love and all. I was happy about everything. There was nothing in my life I could seriously complain about. To me, life was smooth sailing. Then, BOOM! I'm pregnant. There I was questioning everything: work, vehicle, money, love. Questioning do I have enough for this little kid. Questioning the things I said was enough, but are they truly enough? Was I looking over things in my life just so I wouldn't have to acknowledge them, or was I looking things over just to say I'm good or I'm happy? Damn.... Life was starting to live. All because I was pregnant.

Independent; that was me. Friendly; I was her. Silly, confident, spiritual, talented, intelligent, easy-going type of woman. And there I was stuck in my thoughts. I knew to pray but I didn't want to. Let's be honest. I needed help but I didn't want to ask because everyone already had too much to say.

Side Note: People will talk no matter if you give details or not. There will also be people trying to tell you how you should live your life. The question is: Are you going to let them?

People can only control things in your life when you give them the power to do so.

Back to my story. I'm drowning in my thoughts. My parents were mad. Especially since they didn't like

2

my baby daddy. "You deserve better", they say. My dad wanted me to abort the baby. My mom was crying telling me, "You are not going to drive me crazy". Was the life I'm living considered a happy one?! Only time can tell.

Here I am reflecting on the past 3 years of my life. Why 3 years? Because in those 3 years, I didn't acknowledge anything I was seeing. "Why?", because I didn't want to hurt anyone's feelings. Yes! You can say I was becoming a people pleaser. Denying what I was seeing and what I was feeling. All because I didn't want to hurt anyone's feelings even though my feelings were being dragged through the mud.

In those 3 years. I got cheated on. I dated a guy that was an insincere giver. He would give something, but when things got bad, he would ask for it back. He didn't have a job. He was a spoiled mama's boy. Lord Jesus!! It was bad. He was disrespectful. He felt entitled. DID I MENTION HE DIDN'T HAVE A CAR?

I didn't make it any better because I didn't speak up or say anything. During that time I met and fell in love with my childhood crush. He wanted to be in a relationship. He was EVERYTHING. He had a job, a car, and a place to stay. He was considerate, and caring and he wanted the best for me. But, I turned down my crush.......

Yes. Let's just pause for that bad decision.

I was trying to give that 3-year relationship a try. I knew deep down that it wasn't going to work. So, when I expressed that to my crush, he dropped me like a hot potato!! No calls. No texts. No nothing. I told you I was in love, right? I guess I hurt my own feelings because I didn't want to leave something I knew wasn't going to work for me. I decided to put someone else's feelings before my own.

Side note: We end up hurting ourselves. How?! By denying the truth. People show you who they are. And we are trying to repaint the picture. Hoping for the best knowing things aren't looking up. And we won't change nor move all because of fear. "For God hath not given us the spirit of fear; but of power, and love, and a sound mind." 2 Timothy 1:7 KJV That's what the Bible says. Not me. I told you I was spiritual.

here is no way God planned this for me. There is no way I can be thinking like this. There is no way. I mean no way at all. Where is all this coming from? Is this something I have been suppressing? Is this the real me? Am I worthy of better? I want to stop feeling this way soon. I knew what I had to do but I had to put myself first. No matter the feelings that might be at risk. I just knew this could be IT. I had to get out. Out of the way I was feeling. Out of my head. I have to leave the "what ifs" behind. Not knowing the outcomes nor knowing where to start. I had to do it. Trust me. This didn't happen overnight. This took a while.

CHAPTER 2

TIPPING POINT

I realized that I had been neglecting myself, sacrificing my well-being for the sake of others. I had allowed my fears and insecurities to dictate my choices, and now I stood on the brink of collapse. I was tired of being a marionette, dancing to the tune of expectations. It was time to take back control, to put myself first, but that's easier said than done. Saying no was challenging. And going with my first mind wasn't an easy task. I had to end the 3-year relationship because it was hindering my growth. Change wasn't happening. I was settling. I was okay with just doing the bare minimum. I was even okay with getting the bare minimum. The baby is here and the bare minimum was not good enough.

I had to make a change. In my time of being single. I had a broken heart that needed to heal. I had to admit; that I settled for a lot of things I didn't have to settle for. I didn't have to stay in the relationship for as long as I did. But I did. My choice, my fault.

This time to heal did not feel good. I was alone and taking care of a child by myself. I had to find a way to make money. I couldn't just shampoo hair for the rest of my life.

I started focusing so much on becoming the best

6

mom I could. I figured if I go in full mommy mode how I was feeling about myself would just fade away. So I worked and went to church. That was the routine. Get up and take my baby to daycare. Go to work. Pick my baby up and go home. 6 days out of the week. On the 7th day go to church. Pushing my emotions further and further back. I had to make ends meet by any means necessary.

Emotions don't make money. I was hustling like there was nobody in this world but me who could support my child. I had to get it. I was mean, and sometimes heartless. Nobody could tell me anything because I had to build a wall and make it work. So I thought. I was showing up for everyone but myself. To me, I didn't matter.

I became the advice giver, the hard worker, the super friend, the strong friend, the drinker, the smoker, and yes still in church as if nothing that had been going on was really going on. I had a mask on that nobody could see. I was happy all the time. Super happy. Willing to help everyone but myself. Was this what I considered healing?

Side Note: "Time will heal all wounds," they say. But what they don't tell you is. Time will heal any wound.

With proper care, wounds will heal properly. All wounds cannot be treated the same. Some wounds need intensive care. Others need a cartoon bandage.

Back to the story. This healing process wasn't happening fast enough. And I wasn't patient about it. I was broken. I was mad and I had the "why me "questions. And I didn't want anyone to see it because I didn't want to be called weak. I was doing more damage than I was good. This healing process was going all wrong and I can feel it.

I was in deep denial about my feelings. I lashed out in anger. Conversations can be going on and I put my two cents in about my hurt and my pain. And the conversation wasn't even about that. I just included it. Man, when I say it was bad it was bad.
There I was mad, bitter, and lonely. I wanted my baby daddy to hurt just like I was. So I called it out on him. "Can I see my child?" he would ask. My reply was "Nope, you are a liar and I can't trust you".

Every single time. Nope this and nope that. I wouldn't give him a chance. Time went on and things weren't getting better. Until...

 It was an off day and I had no plans for this

particular day. Scrolling on my phone, listening to music about to start my day. I hopped on social media for a quick second. And there it was. A wedding, wedding pictures, family and friends. And my heart dropped. Completely overwhelmed with feelings. My child's father got married and my child wasn't even 1 yet. I sat there and cried my heart out. Tears streamed down my cheeks, hot and heavy. I wept for all the dreams that had crumbled to dust, for the love that had slipped through my fingers like sand. I wept for the person I had lost sight of amidst the chaos; myself. Questions filled my mind and my heart. What the hell? Why in the hell? Why couldn't he marry me? What made her so special? We got a child together. Why didn't he let me know he was dating? And the list went on, and on.

Side Note: Life doesn't stop moving because you are in your healing process. The process of healing is for you. You have to take healing personally.

As I sat there, lost in my sorrow, a gentle breeze seeped through the window, carrying with it the scent of freshly brewed coffee and cinnamon. The fragrance wrapped around me like a comforting embrace, reminding me of simpler times, of moments of peace and contentment.

Slowly, a sense of calm began to settle over me. The intensity of my emotions ebbed, replaced by a quiet acceptance. I realized that escape was not the answer. I needed to face my present, to confront the pain and sorrow head-on. Then, while I was standing in the kitchen God reminded me who I was because I was going down a path I didn't have to. I don't have to. I didn't have to. That phrase echoed in my brain like a relentless drummer drowning out all else. I didn't have to. I didn't have to abandon my dreams, to settle for this life of mediocrity, where days bled into identical blurs and the mundane of routine numbed my soul. I didn't have to, a voice whispered in my ear, and it was the only thing that kept me going, a flicker of hope in an endless sea of monotony.

Then, it all hit me one night. I was at church and I was praying internally. This lady came and hugged me and said "God already forgave you. Now it's time for you to forgive yourself and move on. " Was I punishing myself? I was stuck and didn't realize I was doing it to myself. I denied myself the ability to be myself because of pain, but not any longer. With a newfound sense of purpose, I stepped forward, ready to embrace the beauty and the pain, the joy and the sorrow, the highs and the lows that life has to offer. I

was no longer afraid to be myself. And the best is yet
to come so I thought.

CHAPTER 3

DETOURS TO DESTINY

Do you remember what it felt like when you loved yourself wholeheartedly? My answer is yes, I remember her. I filled my hurt and pain with sex. And I mean real good sex, that was a good pain distraction for me. No feelings were involved as long as I could. No conversations, no connections, you didn't care about me, and I didn't care about you. Until I got told by a guy I am a toxic person and I'm playing with his feelings. He told me " he is not a toy, and he is not my little bitch."

Man, when I tell you my feelings were hurt because, for one, I would have never thought he would talk to me like that. Plus men do it all the time. I'm shielding my heart by any means necessary just like they do. This had to stop. I cut it all off every relationship, sex-ship. Because I can't be no man, I can only be me. A Lady.

So I went through this period of loneliness, and solitude. Quiet time getting to know me all over again. Giving myself boundaries. Loving myself, affirmation, talking positively, doing things I actually like doing. Listening to that positive voice in my head.

At first, it wasn't comfortable because I'm used to

being around people. And I was curious as to why feeling weird about this faze in my life. This faze is calling me to be real with myself. This faze is causing me to ask the hard questions. I needed answers and I had to ask someone that would tell me the truth regardless. That person was my mom. I cringed at the thought.

My mom, Man, that lady is amazing. She always taught me and my sister that we can talk to her about anything. We can come to her about anything. She also warned us that if we do come to her that means we are ready for the answer she will give. I took that to heart. I carried that throughout my life. Honestly, deep down it also made me nervous.

My mom is a strong woman. She knew how to express herself very well. She was the type of woman that didn't just throw her opinions on you. The only way you could know her thoughts or her opinion; you had to ask. So with that being said, you can say I was a little intimidated. She spoke with passion and authority.

She would gaze in your eyes as she talked just so you know she means everything she is saying. That's how I grew up. Knowing all this she was the perfect person to talk too.

She would gaze in your eyes as she talked just so you know she means everything she is saying. That's how I grew up. Knowing all this she was the perfect person to talk to.

As I swallowed my pride I went into my parents room and asked my mom. "Hey momma, am I gullible?"

Side Note: When talking to someone. You have to talk to someone that isn't jealous of you. Someone that will be honest. Someone that can hurt your feelings with love. You just have to put your pride aside to hear the words and accept the truth.

"Momma, am I gullible?" That lady looked at me and answered "Yes." She didn't say anything else. So I was led to ask another question. But I walked out first to gather myself. I went and looked up the definition.

Gullible- easily persuaded by something.

So I went back and I asked how??
She told me you believe everything that you are told

without question. So I asked isn't that good? She replied not all the time, some things in life call for questioning. She proceeded to tell me, "People know that you are going to just take their word for whatever they say". I had to listen with my ears, and my head, and also be honest with my heart. I had to take accountability.

What she was saying wasn't wrong. My heart wanted it to be wrong honestly because I believe everyone deserves a chance. But nobody deserves to hurt your heart twice. Nobody deserves to lie to you twice. Is the question wrong? In my mind no, how are you going to know when you don't ask the question? In my heart, I don't want to be nosy. I want them to know I trust them. My mind and my heart go back and forth.

My mind won this particular battle and it was okay.

CHAPTER 4

OUT

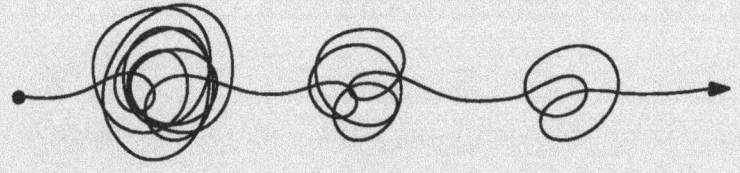

Everything up to this point has been about choices and taking accountability for my actions. None of it was easy but for things to change, I had to make myself do things differently. I needed a different routine, something I knew I could do. So I started with something different. One day I didn't wanna listen to music or watch TV. I didn't want to hear anything. So I took a drive. Listening to the wind, the cars, the road, and letting my mind run free. It was different and comforting. How? I don't know. It just felt refreshing for some reason. At first, it felt weird because why would I drive with the radio off? Nobody was there to judge me. So I was doing the most. I was thinking too deeply.

Side Note: Doing something different causes you to look at yourself differently and you'll notice things about yourself you didn't see before.

It went from no music to just jazz. Cooking with jazz felt good. I read devotional texts in the morning to start my day. My morning routine went like this. Alarm to wake me up 30 minutes before I get my baby up for school. I wake up earlier so I can pace myself. My music softly plays in the room. Go to the bathroom while I'm collecting myself. I read my devotion. When I'm done reading, brush my teeth and wash my face. In the bathroom, I set an alarm to make sure I read everything I needed to read before I left the bathroom. I had to master this! Some days I wasn't in the mood. But I did it anyway. It started to feel worth it when I recognized my baby singing the songs I would play in the mornings. Not only was he singing them. Some days I didn't want to play the music he would ask about it. Not knowing it was putting me back on track.

Side Note: God has a way of showing you. You are on the right track and keep doing what you are doing. The key is you have to be listening.

I'm getting it together. Now the time came when I wanted to go out but nobody was available. My best friend was busy. My sister was out of town. My cousin was working. And I didn't want to go out alone. So I called everyone and left them ALL voicemails. That went a little like this, "I will no longer wait on you to make time. If you can't go I'll be going by myself. You will not stop my day. If I wait on you I'll never get anything done." Who knew it was time for me to eat my words? Shit. So I closed my eyes, took a deep breath, and got dressed. I had no restrictions! I couldn't handle it. It took me forever to get dressed. I didn't know what to wear. I didn't know where to go. I was a mess. I laid down. I got up. I walked back and forth in and out of the kitchen. Up and down the hallway. The outfits changed over and over and over again.

When I noticed I was doing too much. I walked into the bathroom. I looked at myself in the mirror and started asking myself, "Where do you wanna go? What do you wanna do? Do you wanna be cute doing it?!" I told myself, "You don't have to do anything but it has to be your choice. Please don't make your decision based on whether you're going to have company or not." I began to remind myself, "You can eat what you want Shine. You can even cook whatever you want. You can go anywhere you want. You work hard. Your bills are paid. It's okay to treat yourself. Wear whatever you want. Be cute or not. It's your choice. Be comfortable. I had to reroute the way I was thinking. And it was getting easier. I still haven't gone to the movies alone..... oh yeah Netflix.

Life was looking up. Yes, I have failed some days but I didn't wallow in it. I got back up and started again. I was getting my momentum back. I was going to be proud of myself again. I wasn't just living life. I was actually living my life. Enjoying my life. Bumps and bruises hurt but they are also a lesson. There was a point in my life where I thought I was the only one going through. I thought no one would understand. But when you get out of your head. You begin to see there are too many people on the earth to think you are the only one who has experienced what you are experiencing right now. There is someone who has gone through and came out on top. Someone has lived your story and survived. We help one another. Meaning sharing is caring. Your life doesn't have to end in despair. You don't have to stay in anything uncomfortable. You don't have to continue thinking the way you are thinking. You don't have to wait for others to validate you. You don't have to meet the standards of other people. Yes, that includes family. Pace yourself. Live your life. Make yourself smile. One day at a time. One moment at a time. And don't forget God.

You're not alone. There is ALWAYS a way out.